LIKE GRASS, LIKE ATOMS, LIKE YEARS

Like Grass,
Like Atoms,
Like Years

POEMS

J.R. SOLONCHE

Cover design by Jacob Arms
William K. Lawrence, Editor in Chief
Published by Serving House Books
Lawrence Landing Company
Raleigh, North Carolina 27609
United States of America

www.servinghousebooks.com

Serving House Books is a proud member of

Independent Book Publishers Association
 and
Community of Literary Magazines and Presses

Paperback ISBN: 9781947175327

CONTENTS

Part II

Part I

ORPHEUS

He sang for the trees, and the trees swayed.
He sang for the rocks, and the rocks moved closer.

He sang for the wolves, and the wolves lay down.
What's an understatement, you ask?

This is an understatement.
He sang for his wife, Eurydice.

He sang all the way to the underworld,
singing his songs for the living and the dead.

He sang for the ferryman and for the three-headed dog.
He sang his grief into the dark.

And Hades, the King of the Dead, heard the song.
He said, "You can have her back, but you can't look."

All he had to do was look straight ahead.
Walk and she will follow him.

It was a simple instruction.
It was also an impossible instruction.

So he walked.
He walked through the shadows.

He walked through the silence.
He thought he heard her footsteps behind him.

He thought he heard her breathing.
He thought he felt her presence like a ghost.

The impossible part was that he was still alive.
He was filled with doubt.

It was an impossible instruction.
Just before the light, just before the end of the long
dark road, he turned.

And that was that.
A look.

A glance.
And she was gone.

Not a god or a hero could have done it.
Not a hero, not a god.

And he was neither.
He just knew how to sing.

MONASTERY TALES

The Lawn

The master and student are walking past a perfectly manicured lawn. The student says, "Such order, such control." The master replies, "The roots have other ideas".

The Cart

A student sees the master in the supermarket pushing an empty cart. "Master," the student asks, "what have you come for?" The master gestures to the empty cart and says, "Nothing. What have you come for?"

The Faucet

The master watches a dripping faucet, one drop at a time. The student grows impatient and says, "Master, it's leaking." "No," says the master, "it is performing its function."

The Broken Glasses

A student brings the master his broken eyeglasses. "Master," he says, "Now I cannot see the truth." The master takes the broken glasses and puts them on. "The truth looks fine from here," he says.

The Haircut

The master gets a haircut. The student says, "Master, you look different." The master runs his hand over his head and replies, "Only on the outside."

The Clock

A clock on the wall has stopped. The student says, "Master, the clock has forgotten the time." The master smiles. "No," he says. "The time has forgotten the clock."

The Cracked Pavement

A student walks with the master and sees a weed growing through a crack in the pavement. "How determined it is to live," says the student. The master kneels to inspect the weed. "Is it more determined than the pavement is to be pavement?" he asks.

The Empty Seat

A student and the master are on a train. An empty seat sits across from them. The student says, "It is an empty seat." "It is not an empty seat," says the master. "But no one is sitting in it," the student says. "Not so. The two of us are sitting in it now," the master says.

The Pen

A student complains to the master, "My pen is leaking."
The master takes the pen and draws a circle. The ink
smears. "The purpose of a pen is to write," the student
says. "What do you see?" the master asks. "I see ink,"
says the student. "So this pen is fulfilling its purpose,"
the master says.

The Squeaky Wheel

The master is sitting in a chair. A wheel on the chair is
squeaking loudly. The student rushes in with a can of oil.
"Master, I will fix the squeak." "And what will we listen
to then?" asks the master.

The Wilted Flower

A student shows the master a flower that has wilted. "It
is dying," the student says sadly. "It was born knowing
how," the master replies.

The Unread Book

A student holds up a book he has not read and asks,
"Master, what knowledge does this hold?"
"It holds the knowledge of a book you have not yet read,"
the master says.

Morning Meeting

The young monk said, "I have a question." The old monk sighed. "Of course you do," he said.

Evening Meeting

The Master said, "If you meet the Buddha on the road, kill him." A student asked, "What if I meet him in the dairy aisle at the supermarket?" The Master said, "Tell him they're out of almond milk."

The Watering Can

A monk is told to water the garden. He has a leaking bucket. When he returns from the well, half the water is gone. He is praised by the master for watering both the garden and the road.

The Nail

On the wall, a single nail. It holds nothing. The master sees it and says, "It is the only nail that is completely free."

The Umbrella

The student complains, "I lost my umbrella." The master says, "You did not lose it. The umbrella has simply found its freedom from you."

The Broom

A monk asks the master, "When I sweep the path, am I sweeping the path, or am I sweeping the self?" The master hands the monk a broom and says, "That's a terrible broom."

The Kettle

The student says, "I understand nothing." The master nods. The student says, "I understand nothing completely." The master turns away to watch the kettle boil.

The Cup of Tea

A student says to the master, "The ancient teachings are like a cup of tea." The master replies, "Yes, but you should still use a saucer."

The Flowers

A monk asks, "Why do the flowers bloom?" The master points to the calendar and says, "It's April."

The Chopstick

The master holds up a single chopstick. "Is this the path to awakening?" The student says, "No." The master says, "Good. Now go wash your rice bowl."

The Door

The student arrives. The master says, "So, you've come for wisdom." The student says, "Yes." The master points to the door. "Then you must leave the way you came in." The student stands up. "But I came in through the door," he says. "Exactly," says the master.

The Answer

The monk asked the Master, "Is there one answer to every question?"
The Master said, "No." The monk started to leave. The Master said, "Yes."

The Sink

A student was washing dishes. He asked his Master, "Why do we always run out of spoons?"
The Master put down his bowl. "Perhaps we simply have too many hands." The student washed his hands.

The Pear

A monk brought the Master a perfectly ripened pear. The Master took a bite and said, "Delicious." The monk then offered him an unripe pear. The Master took a bite and said, "Delicious." Finally, the monk brought him a rotten pear. The Master took a bite. "Well," he said, "at least it's not a peach."

The Mop

The Master was drinking tea. A disciple walked in and spilled a cup of water. The Master looked at the puddle on the floor. "Don't just stand there," he said. "Get a mop." The disciple asked, "Is that all there is to it?" The Master drank his tea.

Nothingness

A visitor at the monastery asked, "How do you achieve a state of nothingness?" The Master was putting away books. He said, "I used to know. But then I lost the list."

The Leaf

The Master took a broom and began sweeping the leaves from the path. A student pointed to a leaf still on the path and asked, "What about that one?" The Master looked at the leaf. "It knows what it's doing," he said.

The Difference

A visitor at the monastery asked a student, "What's the difference between a student and a master?" Before the student could answer, the master, looking straight at the student, said, "About 40 years."

The Napkin

The student asked, "Where does the thought go when you stop thinking it?" The master picked up a napkin from the table. "Here," the master said, holding it in his hand. Then he threw the napkin away.

The Dog

The student asked, "Does a dog have the Buddha-nature?" The master looked at the dog sleeping by the door. "Yes," the master said, "and it knows better than to answer you."

SHOT

I went for my flu shot today.
I had to fill out a form first.
The last question was, "Are
you feeling anxious about
getting a flu shot today?"
I checked, "No." Because I
do things like this, I asked
the pharmacist what would
happen if I checked, "Yes."
"I'd send you across the street
to the Hook & Ladder Bar
for a pre-shot of Jack Daniels,"
he said. Too bad I had already
checked, "No." Too bad it was
ten o'clock in the morning.

O EARTH, YOU FLIRT!

Flashes of bright yellow
from the kitchen window
catch my eye. They're
the Stella d'Oro daylilies
in their second flowering.
"Look at me," brags
the earth in her brassiest
gold and honey voice.
"Look," she says. Isn't
she sweet? Isn't she sassy?

A FLY

A fly is on the window screen
rubbing its head with its hands.
My Russian grandmother used to say
that flies are the alphabet of the forgotten.
I'm sure it's trying to remember a Russian song.

ZHAO LI PAUSES

to rest, for his arthritis
is getting the better of him.
"What's the matter, Zhao Li?"
asks his arthritis. "I need to rest
because you are hurting me,"
Zhao Li says. "I'm only doing
my master's work," arthritis says.
"Your master?" "Yes, Time's work."
"But Time is an illusion." "Well,
if that is true, then pain is also an
illusion." "Yes, of course. Thank
you for reminding me," Zhao Li
winces, continuing on his way.

HAY WAINS

They sit, a long-married couple,
side by side, in the unkempt, dusty
grass of the field, which they have
forgotten. The field has not forgotten
them. Neither has a crow, a dark,
folded thing, like a thought, perched
on the red one's shoulder. They have
the quiet of things that have been
put away for good, the resignation
of the neglected but dignified old.
A chain, rusted into a circle, sleeps
in the weeds like a loyal dog. And
the air around them, full of the slow
humming life of roots and insects
and small, burrowing animals, moves
in and through the empty spaces
where their souls used to be.

WHY I QUIT FISHING

It taught me something
about patience and stillness,
but my heart wasn't in it.
I sold the rods and reels,
the tackle box, the battery,
the electric motor, the anchor
and the net. I kept the boat
and the oars for a while, so
I could go out on the lake
to practice what I had learned.
I finally gave it to my friend,
Jeff, bless his heart, which is in it.

A ROOSTER

A rooster does not know a lot,
but he knows the important stuff.
He knows he's a *he* and not a *she,*
and he knows why. He lets them
know he knows, and he lets you
know he knows. I hear him every
morning as if from another time
when things were simple. For him,
they still are. He doesn't know he's
obsolete. He crows just the same,
and he knows why. His red comb
is a furious little flag, a declaration
of independence from the 21st century.

EDEN

The fruit looked good. It had to.
It was fresh. It was brand new.
It was the first stab at fruit.
Where on the tree was it? Was it
low-hanging fruit? No, that's too
easy. It was on the highest branch,
the one the snake had to grab and
pull down for Eve to reach. He
still had hands and legs remember.
Anyway, God tells them not to.
And the snake. He's not a monster.
He doesn't frighten them off. He's
not supposed to. He's the tempter.
He's just a creature with an opinion.
He just has a different take on things.
Afterward, the leaves did not so much
cover them as make them aware
that something needed covering.
This is not so much a punishment
as a new kind of idea. Perhaps a new
kind idea is in itself a punishment,
a punishment for those with no need
for any ideas at all and who should
have lived blissfully happily forever
after. And the gate is not a great,
bronze, terrifying thing. It is small.
You can walk right through it. And
the garden is still there, behind you.
The trees are still there. The fruit, all

but one, is still there forever ripe. And
the air that still smells like forever.
The only difference is you know what
forever means now, the real punishment.

ACHILLES

He was born to be the best. And
he was, mostly. He had a great
temper and a love that looked
like all the others until it wasn't.
First, the girl. Then, his pride.
He sits in his tent while the war
he was born to fight goes on
without him. He is a man who
has decided not to be a god.
And so, becomes a bigger one.
When the news comes, it is
small and awful, a fallen friend.
His pride becomes a hollow
thing, a drum that has been broken.
And so he stands up. He goes back
to the war. But not for the war and
the glory. He goes for the smallness,
for the awful thing, for the hollow
drum. The story tells us about the heel,
about the arrow. But it does not tell us
that he no longer cared. We must
read between the lines for that.

SISYPHUS

It's the punishment of punishments.
It's the one worse than death.
It's the first one we think of after
we think of hell. He must roll
that rock up that hill. And when he
gets to the top, it rolls back down, and
he has to start again. I don't know
about this. The rock is a rock. The hill
is a hill. He knows the rock. He knows
the cracks and the rough places. He knows
the little bumps and protrusions. He knows
the way it wants to lean to the right. Or
to the left. He knows the hill. He knows
every stone and every root. He knows
every place where the ground is soft after
a rain. He knows every place where
the sun has turned the dirt rock hard.
He knows every square inch. How could
he not? He hasn't lost his memory, has
he? He's the poet of rocks. He's the poet
of hills. It's a job. It's just a routine, and
if nothing else, he's the poet of routine.
It's another day at the office only
with a better view.

BASHO

Again to the pond
        No frog this time
                No sound of water

Was it a dream?
        Sound of frog and water?
                Or is now the dream?

Three ghosts gather —
        Basho – Frog – Pond
                Old friends sing

Nothing is ever captured.
        So is nothing — O
                ever recaptured.

Who will remember
        Basho except
                that path — that frog

After 1,000 poems
        one frog – one pond – one
                plop — is all

One million stars
        Only one moon
                O all right

POCKET WATCH

I miss my pocket watch.
That doesn't mean I'm going
to buy another one. I'm not.
I don't need one now. I needed
one to get to class on time when
I taught. I needed to take it out
of my pocket and place it on
the desk to show the students
who was in charge of their time.
Me and not the clock on the wall.
It was also a prompt for writing,
a way to get their imaginations
fired up. It was history in real time.
It was time keeping from another
time. It was the time of a train,
the time of a secret, the time of
one waiting for something. The lid
sprang open. The face was familiar,
the face of a relative I heard stories
about but never met. Its tick was
a small heart. It said, *I'm still here.*
When time was up and I put it back
in my pocket, sometimes it was time
well spent, other times not. Their
faces told which it was that time.
Maybe it's not the watch that I miss,
after all. Maybe it's really those faces.

ZIPPO

I quit smoking years ago,
but I still have it, the brushed
stainless steel Zippo lighter.
I like playing with it. I like
the quick metallic snap of it.
I like how it fits in the hand.
It really belongs there. I like
rubbing it with my thumb.
It's more caressing than rubbing.
Some are engraved with names
or dates or mottos or the heads
or wolves or dragons. I never
cared for those fancy ones.
They're not my type. I like
it plain, I like it reliable, I like
it the way I like a woman.

RAIN

Rain falls on the roof.
It's a lot of rain.
It's the sound of
a thousand people
washing their hands at once.

MIRRORS

There are too many fucking mirrors.
There is the mirror that opens
the medicine cabinet above the sink.
That's the first one, and most likely
the one that scares you the most.
There is the magnifying mirror on
the vanity for the fine print of the face.
You keep that one turned to the wall.
Then there is the mirror in the elevator,
the one you almost don't see, but you do.
And the rearview mirror in the car,
which is not for looking at yourself,
but you adjust so you do. And the last one,
the worst of all, the mirror we call the ceiling
in which you see a lifetime of regrets.

A PENNY

I dropped a penny. When I bent
over to pick it up, the man next
to me looked at me like I was crazy.
I get it. It's a stupid penny. It's an
afterthought, not even a thought
at all. I heard it hit the floor, so
I bent over and picked it up without
thinking. It was a reflex. It was
scratching an itch. It's the smallest
of small change. They clutter the
kitchen drawer. The waiter gives
them back when the bill is wrong.
They've been everywhere, more
places than we have ever been.
They belong in piggy banks, in
wishing wells, in Roman fountains.
It's a piece of metal, stamped with
a face that looks familiar. Some of
us still know who it is. We talk of
pennies from heaven. We say a
penny for your thoughts. We say
penny-wise, pound-foolish. We say
my two cents worth. We say heads
is good luck. Mine was tails, but I
picked it up. Why? Because it's
always about something else.

MOTORCYCLES

I have friends who ride motorcycles.
Rob has three, a Triumph, an Indian
and a Russian model with a sidecar
for his wife. Andre wrecked his on
a trip in Alaska. He was badly beat
up, but he's getting a new one. He
says there's nothing he'd rather do
than ride. My brother had a Norton.
He was nearly killed in an accident,
too, but he had the good sense to
give it up. I was on a motorcycle
once in my life. I fell off, but I
was going about four miles per
hour and fell on grass, so I wasn't
injured. And, no, my pride wasn't
injured, either. I've never had much
use for pride, whatever the hell that is.

THE USED BOOKSTORE

The place has a peculiar smell.
It's the smell of used books mixed
with the smell of what the store sold
before it sold used books. I can't
place it. The door has a small brass
bell. The bell knows my name and
announces me to all the books who
look up at me. I recognize many of
them, but their stories are different
now, for they are mixed up with
the stories of the people who have
owned them. Here is a copy of *The
Old Man and the Sea*. Its pages are
stained with something the color of
coffee or tea or for a Hemingway fan,
whiskey. The cover is bent back at
the corner. Clearly, it's been read many
times. Here is *Finegan's Wake*. It looks
pristine, never read, which I perfectly
understand. Here is a book of poems
by a poet I know well. I've been jealous
of the bastard a long time. On the title
page, someone has written in spidery ink,
To my best friend, from her best friend.
So now I can be jealous of that, too.
Because I have to buy something, I buy
a cheap edition of Neruda. There's no
dedication. No reason to be jealous of
that. Besides, I'm not jealous of poets
who write in languages other than mine,
even ones who win Nobel prizes.

SIDDHARTHA GAUTAMA

He had never seen a sick man before.
He had never seen an old man. He had
never seen a dead one. He had never
seen a holy man. This was the way his
father, the king, wanted it. A bubble
of privilege. A limousine with the black
out windows or a house on a cul-de-sac
with the security system always on.
He rode out and saw them. The sick,
the old, the dead, the holy. It bothered
him. It bothered him more than a stone
in his shoe. (He gave up shoes for sandals
and removed those, too, to go barefoot
into a village.) It's an easy thing to see
a dead man. We see them on the news
all the time. But to see your own death,
and your father's death, and the death of
the man who gave you plums, all in one
afternoon -- that's a different thing. That's
the kind of thing that makes you leave.
Not just the palace. Not just the life. That's
the kind of thing that makes you go so far
away you have to change your name.
The kind of thing that makes you sit under
a fig tree for forty-nine days without moving,
resisting every temptation, until you attain
release from suffering. That kind of thing.

RAKING

It has been in the shed
since last November.
The tines are bent. One
is missing. It was cheap,
on sale at the hardware
store. I never thought it
would last this long.
The leaves are already
in piles from the wind.
They look better like that,
more natural, just as any
natural thing should look.
I start raking. Out of spite.
Spite, the last motivation.
Spite, the muse who always
comes when no other sister
does. Besides, what else does
one do with a rake made by
a poor craftsman? Lean on
for a bit, then place on top
of a hill of leaves like some
old and cracked glass jar you
left in the shed for dead?

CROWS

I live in upstate New York, and
it's crow hunting season here.
It makes sense. The farmers hate
them. That's why they put *scare-*
crows in the corn fields and not
scarecardinals or *scarehawks*.
On the telephone wires they look
like notes on a musical staff, a bad
song written for a day that cannot
be trusted. In the trees, they blend
with the shadows. Only when they
caw and take off do you know which
is which. And those caws don't end
with periods or question marks.
They end with exclamation marks.
They declare their presence and dare
you do something about it. So, it
makes sense to blast them out of
the air with a 12-gauge from now
until the end of March. I prefer blue
jays. I like the flash of cobalt and
the call that cuts the crow's caw
down to size. No, I am not a fan
of crows. But I am pretty sure I
understand where they're coming
from. They dare you, and you do,
and they accept you as blood brothers.

IRISH WHISKEY

It's the color of a day I once had
a long time ago. Some say it is
the "water of life," but it is also
the water of forgetting. I lift
the heavy, thick-bottomed glass.
A glass for sitting and thinking,
not for hurrying things, a book
you mean to finish but keep coming
back to the beginning. There's a
secret in it. And a deeper secret
inside of that secret. Some say
it's smoother, less smoky, because
they distill it three times. My friend,
Jeff, who drinks Scotch, says there's
no peat. He says it with a kind of
sorrow, like he's missed a storm.
I tell him to drink the storm, and
I will drink the quiet, secrets and all.

ON KAVANAGH

"The fellow's verse is provincial,"
they said. You said, "Parochial."
Which is not the same thing.
A provincial poet looks over his
shoulder at the metropolis, trying
to make his poems fit in. A parochial
poet doesn't care. He looks at his own
fields, at the bicycles going past in
twos and threes, and finds a universe
in them. So when you died, and they
put a statue of you on the Baggot
Street Bridge in Dublin, it was like
you tricked them. They thought you
were writing about yourself, but really,
you were writing about them. They
just didn't notice that what you found
in Monaghan was what they were
missing in Dublin.

HUNGER

I'm reading Kavanagh's "The
Great Hunger" again, certainly
the greatest poem ever written
about masturbation. He was the
second greatest Irish poet after
Yeats, at least until Heaney came
along. I'm drinking Proper Twelve
Irish whiskey. It's okay, but it's not
Red Breast 25 Year Old, the best or
Dunville's 21 Year Old Palo
Cortado Cask Finish, number two.
Solonche, you fool, what are you
talking about? It's Irish whiskey.
It's Irish poetry. It's masturbation,
for Chrissake.

FIVE JAPANESE DEATH POEMS
IN THE STYLE OF ME

1.
I should have tidied up.
There are books on the floor
and a coffee cup with a half-
moon stain on the bottom.
The window is open,
and a breeze is coming in.
The room will be cleaner later.

2.
My wife always said
I had too many socks.
Some had holes in the toes.
Some were stretched way
out of shape. Today, I am
putting on the best pair I own.
She would have liked that.

3.
The rain is falling
on the window.
The world looks like
it is crying. It's not.
Bless the one person
who will.

4.
I should have said more.
I should have said less.
Either way, it would
have been the wrong
thing. Either way, it would
have been the last thing.
I was driving home.

5.
A turkey vulture crossed
the road. There was no
roadkill in sight. Who
would blame me if I
thought it was going to
be my last drive home?

BETTER GLUE

His son wanted to fly. His father
knew how to make wings. He said,
We won't use wax this time. He used
glue. Strong glue. Industrial glue.
The kind they use for airplanes.
The son said, *What about the sun?*
The father said, *The glue will hold.*
The son said, *What about the sea?*
The father said, *The glue will hold.*
So the son put on the wings.
The father said, *Don't fly too low.
Don't fly too high.* The son said,
*Don't worry, old man. The glue
will hold.* And it did. The son flew.
And the father watched. And he
flew. And he flew. And the father
watched and watched. The son flew
away. He got smaller and smaller.
And the father watched until he
could no longer see the son in the far
distance. He is probably still flying
now, the son. The father sighed.
He almost wept. Perhaps he did weep.
No one knows for sure. The glue held.
The wings held. The son didn't. He
wasn't supposed to. It was good glue.

ECHO AND NARCISSUS

Shouldn't it be Narcissus and Echo?
How could a narcissist tolerate not
being first? Or for that matter, share
billing with anyone else? There's no
way. Let's indulge him. Let's call it
the myth of Narcissus. We all know
the story, but it's so good, it's worth
telling again. He bent down very low,
right down to the water where he saw
something beautiful. He did not know
who it was. A good-looking stranger
who happened to be in the pool below.
She – the anonymous one - stood in
the trees. She said what he said, word
for word for word for word. Although
she had lost her body, she still had her
voice. It was a sad fate, or maybe not.
You could argue the body, even a toe,
gets in the way sometimes. Anyway,
he kept talking to the reflection and
didn't notice the trees or the flowing
voice in the trees. He had a lot of things
to say. All of them important. To him.
The water was calm. He reached out
to touch the beautiful stranger. The water
rippled. And wouldn't you know?
The stranger vanished. He was very
surprised. He tried again. And again.
She kept saying what he said. This went
on until he was turned into a flower,
his own yellow echo and no longer
had need of her.

LEDA

She was out for a walk. Just a simple walk
by the river, as usual. That's the key phrase –
as usual. That's what they did. Go for walks
as usual. It was a nice day, not too hot,
maybe a little cloudy. He was in the form
of a swan. Never tried that one before.
A shower of gold, a bull, but never a swan.
Just a large bird, a big, strong animal,
acting strangely. She was a princess,
but a princess can still be knocked off her
feet. But she was also a queen so should
have known better. Anyway, she went home
and told her husband, King Tyndareus.
What could he say? You can't really get mad
at a god, especially when he's already gone.
So she laid the eggs. That's what you do.
You just make do with what you've got.
And the children hatched, two from one,
two from the other. One set was his.
The other set was hers and her husband's.
The difference was like something you know
and something you just have to live with.

ODYSSEUS

In the hall he finds a bow no
one can string. The suitors
laugh. They're drunk. They
trip on the carpet. They do not
know this is his house. He has
been away for a very long time.
He once told a cyclops his name
was No One. He once listened
to women who wanted to kill
him with a song. Now, he is
just a stranger in his own
living room. For twenty years,
Ithaca had heard only the noise
they made. Only the shouting,
only the clattering of plates, only
the scraping of chairs. He picks
up the bow, and the suitors stop
laughing, and the room is as
silent as wax in the ears. The man
of the house is home.

HECTOR

He was a good father. He was
a good husband. He was a good
brother. This is what they say.
He went out to fight Achilles,
and he knew what would happen.
He was a good husband, but
Andromache watched from
the tower, and he could see her
from the plain, a small, dark
shape. He knew what would
happen. He left his wife and
his son. His small son, terrified
of his father's bronze helmet.
His son, whose name was a
question, *Astyanax*. He knew
what would happen to his son.
But he had to fight. It was what
he did. It was who he was. So
he went out to meet the man who
was his own fate. He knew what
would happen. And the gods sat
on Olympus, the gods and the
goddesses, they watched him die.
Just like we watch a movie. Just
like we watch the news. They
knew what would happen.
Hector. The good husband.
Hector. The good father. Hector.
The good brother. He went out

anyway. And what we remember
is that he went out anyway. And
isn't that the tragedy? Isn't the
tragedy always what we always
go out to do anyway?

LOUGHRAN'S

My friend Jeff and I are the same age.
He's a vet. He joined. He went to Vietnam.
I was drafted but was physically unfit.
He talks about it only when he's drunk,
and it's always the same story. His outfit
is dug in in the jungle. They're surrounded
by VC. He's scared. They're all scared.
He's trying to remember the code word.
He keeps whispering, "Spaghetti." It's a
word the gooks could never pronounce.
He just keeps whispering, "Spaghetti,
spaghetti, spaghetti." He looks me in
the eye and says, "What's the password?"
"Spaghetti," I say. "No. That's the code
word. Want me to blow you away?
What's the password, jerk?" he says.
He makes a rifle out of his index finger.
"Meatballs," I say. "Okay, pass through,"
he says, turning the rifle back into his
hand and smiling, as though he just won
the war. It's a game. The least I can do
is play -- every time and pay -- every time.

WEEPING CHERRY

I have a weeping cherry tree.
I planted it to replace the peach
tree that was killed by a winter
storm a few years ago. It's an
easy tree. It doesn't cause trouble.
In the spring, it has pink blossoms.
It's a pretty tree, but it's always
weeping. I don't know why it
weeps all the time. The branches
just hang there. They don't reach
for the sky. They don't reach for
anything. It has a kind of dignity.
Is it the dignity of not trying? I
wish I knew what it's weeping
about. It's a secret. And bless its
heart, it's entitled to have one.

BELIEF

When I was young,
I wanted to believe in God.
That didn't last long.

When I was older,
I wanted to believe in love.
That lasted a little longer.

When I was older yet,
I wanted to believe in wisdom.
That lasted even longer.

But there has been nothing
I ever wanted to believe in
more than that time does not exist.

This is why I'm waiting today
for the hummingbirds that left
for Mexico yesterday.

THE REVIEW

The email arrived. The subject line
was just a name. Fredrick Johnson.
The body was a bad review. It wasn't
a mean review. It was just bad. It said
I tried too hard. It said the metaphors felt
like work. For a moment, I felt nothing.
Then I felt a kind of weight. Not a heavy
weight, but a small, leaden thing, like
a paperweight that had fallen onto my
chest. I reread it. *Tried too hard.* The phrase
sat there, like a small uncomfortable chair
in a very long room. I pictured all the drafts,
all the lines that disappeared. I pictured all
the trying. The review was not wrong. Just
unwelcome. I went to the kitchen and made
a sandwich. I do not know why I did this.
Perhaps the small, leaden thing on my chest
had made me hungry. The bread was soft.
The cheese was bland. The tomato too hard.
It did not try too hard to be a sandwich. I ate
the sandwich and did not give it a second
thought. The paperweight was still there, but
it was smaller now, just a little paperweight.
A light-weight paperweight holding down
a paper-thin bad review.

WHY I WANTED TO BE
AN ASTRONOMER

It was not a telescope, or a book
with diagrams of the solar system.
It was not the romance of the stars,
which I only knew from television.
It was the streetlights. I was a boy
in the Bronx, and the streetlights
were a kind of enemy, a kind of
pollution. They were always on,
a yellowish wash over everything,
blurring the edges of the night.
I wanted to be an astronomer, so
I could turn them off. Not all of
them, just the ones between my eyes
and the sky, especially the one right
outside my bedroom window.
I imagined a switch, a master switch,
that would cut the city's yellow glare,
and in that sudden dark, the stars
would rush in, like a crowd in an
empty room. I wanted to find a light
that was not a streetlight, that was
not a porch light, that was so far away
it could not be turned off. I wanted to
know the universe like the back of my
hand. I did not become an astronomer.
I wasn't good enough at math. I became
a poet, and I came to know the universe
of the back of my hand.

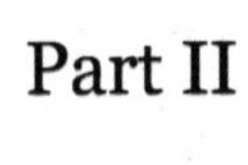
Part II

LIKE GRASS, LIKE ATOMS, LIKE YEARS

There's a big boulder on my lawn.
It's the only one. I like to look at it,
not that it resembles anything
other than a boulder. It's the center
of my attention because it's alone.
I've been looking at it for years.
I looked at it today. I could swear
it looks like it's getting smaller.
I know full well it isn't, unless
it's smaller by an atom's width.
It looks smaller only because
the grass surrounding it is taller.
I guess it's an optical illusion
of sorts, but it really isn't that
either. Yes, it is an illusion but
not an optical one. It's an illusion
like grass, like atoms, like years,
like all the rest is illusion. Like that.

THE FUTURE

Jeff wants to know the future.
That's why he wants to live to
be a hundred. Not for the sake
of living, but so he can see
the future. At least that much of it.
I want to see the future, too. Not
like the prophets did, with their
burning bushes and wild visions
of wars and famines and floods.
Not like the fortune tellers, with
their glass balls. Not like Jeff.
The way you see the sticker you
never peeled off stuck to the back
of the door. I just want to see.
I would like to know if the coffee
stain I made on the oak desk will
still be there. I would like to know
if the weeds I failed to pull from
the garden have grown into a new
kind of wilderness. All the small
things that had my fingerprints on
them. I do not care about the wars.
I do not care about the popes. I just
want to know if the door, the one
with the sticker still on it, will still
close the same way it does now.

WAITING

Waiting for death is a waiting
unlike any other. When you wait
at the bank, you know you will
leave after you get the cash. When
you wait at the traffic light, you
know you will go again on green.
When you wait in the dentist's
office, you know you will leave
after the filling. When you wait
for the train, which will be late
because it always is, nevertheless,
you know you will home for dinner
even if it might be cold. Waiting
for death is not this. Waiting for
death is a different kind of waiting.
Waiting for death has no *when*.
Waiting for death has no *after*.
Waiting for death has no *again*.
Waiting for death has only *know*.
Waiting for death has only *now*.
Waiting for death has only *no*.
Waiting for death has only *O*.

LIBRARY

A teenager came into the library.
She was wearing headphones,
music loud enough that I could
hear the beat in my teeth. I felt
like telling her to turn it off or
turn it down. I didn't because
she made me think of what I used
to do in college, cutting classes
to spend all my time in the library
listening to Arturo Toscanini
conduct the NBC Symphony play
Siegfried's "Rhine Journey" and
"Funeral Music" on the record player
over and over. It was so loud through
the headphones, the librarian had to tap
me on the shoulder to get me to turn
it down, which all the other students
hearing the beat in their teeth should
have thanked me for.

GLASSES

Glasses, my glasses, what
are you? More than an old
friend, much more. You're
a body part I wasn't born
with but need to survive, the
eyes my eyes weren't up to
doing. There on the night table,
you look like a rusted old bike
on a hill in a haze. I put you
on, and the world comes into
focus. Again. The way it is in
my dreams, the details sharp
and clear, the colors vivid and
the room becomes a real place
again, and I, a real person again
who has to face it all again.

CIVILIZATION

Convicts in Maine prisons
do not make license plates.
They make wood furniture.
Fine wood furniture. Tables,
chairs and such. They fetch
high prices up there. It doesn't
take much to be civilized.

THE BEST MEDICINE

My friend Charlie is my doctor.
He likes to say, "Laughing is
good for the heart." He even
quoted a study that claims that
laughing 100 times is equal to
10 minutes on the rowing machine
or 15 minutes on an exercise
bike. That's fine. "But crying is
twice as good as laughing because
it's good both for the heart and
for the soul," I tell him. He agrees
that crying can be a healthy release,
but he cautions that it can have side
effects like puffy eyes and sinus
pressure. It can also be perceived
negatively if done frequently or in
certain social settings. "Don't worry,
doc. I'm a poet. I cry only while
I'm laughing," I say. He laughs.

TO MY NOSE

Thank you, nose, for
coming forward going
forward when my eyes
failed me so soon at six
and for being there in the
thick of things to carry
my glasses on your own
shoulders. My ears do
their part, it's true, but
you, my nose, you do
the lion's share. You are
the tireless one, the Atlas
who holds up all I behold.

MOONLIGHT

I get up in the middle of
the night. The full moon
at the window lights my
way down the stairs. When
I come up, I close the blinds.
I have a problem with full
moons. They may light my
way to the bathroom, but
they don't let me sleep.
And if they do, they give me
bad dreams. "Here," they say.
"Take these bad dreams. We
offer them on silver platters.
Who else is as generous?"

ROSES

I wrote a poem about roses.
I wrote what everyone has
written. How beautiful they
are. How fragrant they are.
I read it to them. They laughed.
They've heard it all before.
They've heard it in Persian, in
Greek, in Mandarin, in French,
in German, in English, in every
language with a word for them.
So they laughed at me. That was
fine with me. I like audiences to
laugh, especially when they're
beautiful and fragrant, when
they smell like roses.

THE EARTH NEVER FAILS
TO SURPRISE

The earth never fails to surprise,
such as this new wisteria
vine twisting its way, tenaciously up,
tenderly up, up the same tree its mother, years
ago, let go of and fell from.

VIEW OF A LAKE

It is widest in winter,
which is when the trees
to your right and left
are leafless, but when
it is cold enough, as it
always becomes, you
are left looking right
ahead at ice, a lake for
all intents and purposes,
lifeless in dead silence.

WILD TURKEYS

They come from the woods
when – what? – they feel
like it, the turkeys, wild as
the woods, dark as the woods
on moonless nights and cross
the black road, disappearing
into it as they cross it, only to
disappear again into the woods
on the other side, which was
the same woods when there
was no other side.

SEASONAL

Caught between summer
and winter, I feel for spring
and fall, for they must choose
which one each prefers, which
the brother, which the sister,
wants to live with at the divorce
of mother and father. Bewildered.
Bewildered. So the sister will go
with mother, so the brother will
go with father. Unfair. So unfair
to them, to spring and fall.

BLUE

The sky is a sheet of blue paper.
Not any blue. Not every blue.
Sky-blue, solid, uninterrupted.
A blank check there for you fill
out with the amount your day
is worth. A day with no clouds
is like a person with no worries.
But I have questions. Where are
all the ships? All the galleons?
All the dragons? All the whales?
All the ghosts of our best intentions?
But I feel good for the sky. Really.
It deserves to have a worry-free day
once in a while. I'll do the worrying
for it. I'm good at it. I'm the best.

THE DIFFERENCE

The breeze is what we invite.
It comes in the window with
the scent of newly cut grass
or yesterday's rain. We smile
at the breeze because we have
asked it in. We want it to stay
a while. The wind is different.
It's a bad relation. It has a record.
It comes with a warning. It rattles
the glass. It has something to say
that we would rather not hear.
The wind is not invited. We do not
smile at the wind. We can't. It
would wipe it right off our faces.

OPHELIA

They said she was mad. The way
the trees go mad when the wind
has its way with them. The branches
all askew, the leaves muttering
nonsense. But she was never a tree.
She was a flower. A flower plucked
by one who knew what a hand was for,
when to close it, and when to thrust
a sword with it. The stream doesn't
care about madness. Nor does it care
about sadness. What it knows is weight.
The weight of a dress, the weight of
a secret. She wasn't singing. She was
taking notes, which sounded like singing.
And when she was done, she left them
there. On the surface of the water. A gift.

KING HAMLET

He is what's left when a thing
is broken. A king with only
one subject, his son, the prince.
And so he visits his son, who
is having a worse time of it
than he is, who wishes he's dead.
At least back in school, far away
from the rottenness of Denmark.
He watches him try to fix things.
He wants to grab him by the lapels.
He wants to shake him. He wants
to give him a swift kick in the ass.
But a ghost has no hands. He can
only speak, and he's running out
of words, and he runs out of words,
until his son, the prince, who has never
run out of words, runs out of words.

ADVICE

A student asks Zhao Li if he
has advice for an aspiring young
poet. "No, I don't have advice for
an aspiring young poet such as
yourself, but I do have advice for
a retiring old poet," Zhao Li says.
"Well, since someday I will be such
a retiring old poet, could you give it
to me now, Zhao Li?" asks the student.
"Yes, here is my advice. Never take
advice from poets," he says waving
the student away.

VAN GOGH'S LAST PAINTING

The last thing he saw, they said,
was the wheat field and the crows.
Dark strokes. Heavy sky. A drama
that made sense to those who knew
how the story ended. But that was
not the last. The last was not a field
of gold. The last was not a sky. He
wasn't looking up. He wasn't looking
away. He was looking down. He was
looking in. It was the earth, the ground.
The roots of a tree, exposed, gnarled,
twisting on a slope along a road in
Auvers-sur-Oise. He didn't finish it.
He was tired. He would come back.
So he left it there, against the fence,
or next to a field. The last thing he
saw was not crows leaving a field,
but a tree reaching down to earth,
and the earth, expectantly willing,
waiting to embrace her lover.

THE BUDDHA ON MY
NEIGHBOR'S LAWN

It is a concrete Buddha, not
a stone Buddha. Or perhaps
it is a heavy plastic Buddha.
I've never seen it up close,
but I think it is concrete. It
should be something made
of sand. Either way, it sits
there, with a pig-like paunch,
cross-legged, on the lawn,
under a tree, not meditating.
Observing, amused. Perhaps
observing is also meditation.
And amusement must be. The
mower goes around it without
disturbing it. Every day is
the same day for the Buddha,
while for the lawn it is a day
of being cut, then growing,
being cut again, growing
again, being cut. The Buddha
does not change. The lawn does.
The lawn changes and changes
as my neighbor mediates and
meditates in wider and wider
circles away from the tree
in smaller and smaller circles.

HAIRCUT

It is a small thing, getting a haircut.
Not a big, life-changing thing. Not
a birth or a death. Not an earthquake
or the changing of a season. She puts
the cloth around your neck, a flimsy
cape. Something you might wear if
you were a small superhero with a small
power. The small talk is sharp, quick.
The snip, snip of scissors. The weather.
The traffic. The hairs fall to the floor,
each one a miniature version of the hair
you had just a minute ago. They're all
the commas you cut from the essays
your students wrote over twenty-five
years. You get a little shorter. And when
you leave, the wind feels like a different
season on your neck. And your head is
ready for the hand of your dreams upon
it. Ready for the earthquake you've been
waiting for to change the rest your life.

OCTOBER

The lake is full of them now.
Honking and flapping.
Canada geese.
The gathering of the tribes.

A splendid excitement.
An urgent commotion.
They get ready to move on.
They practice, rehearse.

Not the last one.
Not the dress rehearsal.
They haven't yet done full *V* full dress.
That's coming soon.

They get into their formations.
Elders ahead.
Juveniles behind.
Each in its proper position.

To survive.
To succeed, which means to survive.
I watch them and admire.
I watch them and envy.

It is cold and getting colder
as I stand and watch them in the air
of this troubled and disordered world.
And I despair.

QUESTIONS FOR TODAY

Was it a good day to get up?
Was the coffee hot enough?
Was it in the right cup?
Did the dream make you laugh?

Why wasn't the cat waiting for you?
Was the floor cold under your feet?
Now what were you going to do?
Did the dream make you weep?

What was the first thing you heard?
Was it the rain?
Was it a bird?
Was it your arthritis pain?

Were you going to go back to bed?
Did you keep one, just one promise to the dead?

ANSWERS FOR TODAY

I both laughed and cried.
I've never tried it.
A million were born and a million died.
I did but she denied it.

That was a long time ago.
No one could blame him.
Yes, I know, I know.
He did it on a whim.

I wanted to, but I was sick.
Yes, I heard about it, too.
I never liked her kind of music.
Nothing you may have heard is true.

He has an answer for everything.
Shit, that has to sting.

LAZARUS

He came out of the tomb,
still wrapped up. He blinked
like a man waking from a nap.
Blinded, he shielded his eyes
against the sun. They all stared,
his sisters, the disciples, the crowd.
Even Jesus stared. He rubbed his
eyes, amazed by his own miracle.
They had their questions ready.
What is it like? What did you see?
He said nothing. He just stood
there. He just looked at the one
who said, "Lazarus, come out."
It was such a loud voice, the
loudest voice he had ever heard.
Jesus was his close friend. Why
would he do this unspeakable
horror to him? His mouth was dry.
He was thirsty. He was hungry.
He was weak. He could barely walk.
Later, at the table, they asked again.
What is it like? What did you see?
He just took another piece of bread.
He just took another sip of wine.
He just kept turning to his friend,
sitting next to him who just kept
filling his cup. There was no great
secret. Only the sound of swallowing.

USE

The woman at the hardware store
said, "Can I help you?" as I wandered
down an aisle of paint brushes "No,
thank you," I said. What I really needed
was a different kind of brush, one that
could cover the cracks in my memory.
She moved on to another customer,
someone who actually knew what they
came for. But the question stuck with
me, a fleck of paint on a thumb. "Can I
help you?" Help with what? The years
piled up, drying paint cans on the shelves
of my brain, and none had the right color.
Some were labeled, *The Summer of '82.*
Others, *My Daughter's Laugh.* Most were
just a vague, unhelpful shade, like "off-
white" or "beige." I picked up a brush,
a cheap one and held it up to the light.
It felt useless. I felt useless. I bought it
anyway just for the sake of having done
something. "I see you found what you
were looking for," she said as I paid.
"Yes," I said. Her smile was useful.
It was exactly what I was looking for.

THE KNIFE

He thought about the morning walk.
The dust on Isaac's sandals, the small
talk on the way up the mountain.
The boy's voice, like a little stone
rolling down a slope. Abraham must
have coughed then, and looked at the sky,
which was blue and empty. Yahweh
not in sight. He thought about the knife.
The flint knife, the sacred knife, the one
he used for circumcisions, the one he
used on himself and on his son, the one
he would again use on his son. It was
sharper than any iron. It had to be. He
prayed his hand would not fail him.
And the voice, the voice that had spoken,
was it his own? The wind in the dry grass?
And he came down the mountain, holding
his son by the hand, such a small, white
hand. Would it hold the knife steady
when he brought it down on Jacob?

THE DUST

The dust of the field gets in your
clothes, it makes a dry film on
your skin, it settles in the creases
of your palm. One morning, Cain
walked into the field. His brother,
Abel, walked with him. It was an
ordinary morning, like any other.
The voice had come to him before,
when the smoke of his offering hung
low to the earth, stubborn and gray.
His brother's smoke always rose clean
and straight, a slender ribbon of praise,
and that was the problem. The voice
in his head said, *Not good enough.*
The other voice, the one outside,
the one from the sky, said, *You can
master it.* He thought about that.
Master it. But how do you master
a thing that lives in your bones like
a hunger? The dust on Abel's feet
was the same as the dust on his own.
He thought about that, too. They were
from the same ground, came from
the same place, made of the same clay.
But the dust on Abel's hands was clean.
His own hands, always in the soil,
were stained, the way all hard work stains

a man. He saw the difference, and he could
not bear it. And so the dust drank what it
was thirsty for, and his brother's blood
was crying out from the ground. And
he knew he would someday join him.

LIFE

I went into Bank Square
Coffee for coffee. While
the barista was drawing
a perfect white leaf in
the center, I dropped a
five in the tip jar. "I see
you must a graphic arts
major," I said. "No, it's
English, actually," she
said. I added another five.

ART APPRECIATION

van Gogh is my favorite
painter, but whenever
I take my glasses off,
all I see is Monet. I asked
my ophthalmologist
what she could do about
it. "Change your favorite
painter," she said.

ROSES

There used to be roses.
They came with the house.
They were part of a garden,
but the garden was already
all but gone by then. They
were surrounded, strangled
by the scrub and tangled
bramble. They were wild,
small, red, not full-blooded
but an anemic, bulimic red.
The thorns fit right in, born
for that kind of world, that
kind of life. Nevertheless,
for a time, I waded in to cut
those flowers I could get to.
My fingers bled for them,
even through my gloves. We
had a pact, blood-sisters and
blood-brother, the roses and
I, but my blood was not their
blood, and they shriveled,
and they died.

ADVICE TO A YOUNG POET

Do not write about the sky,
or what the clouds look like.
Instead, write about the ceiling.
The crack in the plaster. That
is the real sky. For God's sake,
do not write about love. Write
about the way she puts her car
in reverse, the way she turns
her head, the way her hair (O,
her hair!) sways, the way
the brake lights leave a wake
of blood. That is the real love.
Do not write about a mountain.
Write about the pebble in your
shoe that makes you want to
stop walking. That is the real
mountain. So, go ahead and
write but not about big things.
Write about small things, how
the refrigerator hums a sad
refrain, the way the milk
carton sweats on the table,
the way the spoon sways in
your hand. Write about that.
All the things that are in your
way. What have you got to lose?

MORE ADVICE TO A YOUNG POET

Do not wait for the muse.
She is a woman, a modern
woman, and she has a life
of her own. Do not wait for
the big idea, the one that
will change the world. The
big ideas are like big fish.
They are caught less often.
Start with a word like "dust,"
or "shoe," or "dog." The word
you were looking at when
you stopped looking for it.
The first word will lead to
the second word, then the
third. This is not a miracle.
It is called writing. You will
not know what you are doing,
not at first. You may not know
what you are doing for a very
long time. Don't worry. The
words do not know either.
They'll figure it out together.
Like old friends with nothing
new to say to each other until
they realize they do. Never
erase. Never cross out. You
may need those words later.
And for God's sake, never
marry a poet.

THE TAPE MEASURE

It came to measure for new
blinds, for the old ones were,
well, old and blind. It came
into the living room, into the
dining room, into the bedroom.
I watched it put its metal tip
in the corner of the window
frame, unfurl its strip of metal
to the other corner, and snap
back into its case with a *whir*.
"This one is 36 by 60," it said.
"This one is 36 by 52," it said.
"This one is 32 by 60," it said.
"This one is 32 by 52," it said.
"This one is 36 by 60," it said.
"This one is 36 by 52," it said.
It was measuring an emptiness,
a void, a hole. But it knew what
it was doing. It was taking the
world's measure. It's a poet.

WONDERLAND

I read *Alice in Wonderland*
for the first time since I read
it to my daughter when she
was a child. It is, indeed, a
land of wonders, a land of
wonderful wonders, but the
wonder of wonders is how
that child grew to a woman
in but a single day. And I am
still looking, Oh, still looking,
for the cake crumbs.

WORDS

Some things can only be
undone with a lot of friction.
I had a word to remove.
It felt wrong smack in
the middle of a poem, so
I turned the pencil around
on its little pink ass and
rubbed it back and forth
to remove the thing, put it
out of its misery. The words
around the space looked
worried. "Are we next?" they
wondered. "No," I reassured
them. "Look, here's the new
one." "Ah, yes. Thank you.
We can live with that," they
beamed up from the page.

FLAGS

Two of my neighbors fly flags.
Neither one knows anything
about the protocol for American
flags. They leave them out all
the time, in all kinds of weather,
day and night. The reds have
faded to a washed-out pink,
the blues to a hazy lilac. Torn
here, ripped there. They look
sad. It is sad to see them looking
so sad. They don't seem to care.
Or maybe they want them to look
like they've been through a war.
Are they warning me that a war
is coming? A civil war? I doubt it.
They're not that clever. The flags
are just pieces of cloth hanging on.
They're just a couple of limp dicks.

CITY ZEN

The Diner

The waiter asks, "What would you like?" The man says, "What I had yesterday." The waiter pauses, looks out the window, and replies, "You cannot have it."

The Park

An old man sits on the park bench watching pigeons. "What are you doing?" I ask. "Waiting," he says. "For what?" I ask. "For them to get tired of it," he replies.

The Museum

The sign says, "Do Not Touch." A child touches it anyway. The child is not punished. The sign, having been touched, is no longer the same sign.

The Street Corner

"The sound of one hand clapping is the sound of my daughter's karaoke machine," one says to the other.

The Street Vendor

The street vendor sells hot dogs as if they are little prayers. He gives each one its due reverence with mustard and onions and a moment of silence before wrapping it in a paper napkin.

The River

The loud voice of a siren fades. The next one takes its place. A river. Is the source the "Lake of Emergencies?"

The Shadow

The shadow of a fire escape ladder. A staircase into the sky. No one climbing, just the shape of escape.

The Message

Someone has written "Forgive me" in the dust on a car window. It is a small, quiet offering. The city offers no reply, only more dust.

The Conversation

The homeless man talks to himself. It is a conversation that must be very interesting since it has lasted so long.

The Cup

The empty coffee cup sits on the park bench. It has had a busy morning, filled with ambition, and now it has found its peace.

The Argument

A couple argues on the sidewalk. Their words are small, sharp stones being thrown. The city, a large, indifferent river, immediately swallows the ripples.

The Heart

The sax player in the subway station plays his heart
out, but the train's heart is bigger.

The News

The newspaper box is empty. The day's events are over.
The emptiness is the longest story of all.

Thoughts

The man in the park is feeding the squirrels. He thinks
he is being kind. The squirrels think he is merely
fulfilling his purpose.

The Umbrella

The broken umbrella in the trash can is a little bit of
failure, a little bit of surrender,
and a little bit of blue sky that will never be seen again.

The Bicycle

The broken bicycle chained to the post is a lesson in
letting go. It is no longer a bicycle.
It is a conversation with the elements.

The Rain

The rain begins again, a long, hushed conversation
between the sky and the city. The city does not reply,
but its windows are listening.

Poetry Books by J. R. Solonche

1965
Letters to Dave
The Consolations
Collected Short Poems
Barren Road
Night Visit
Old
Then Morning
Reading Takuboku Ishikawa
The Architect's House
God
The Eglantine
Alone
The Dreams of the Gods
The Book of a Small Fisherman
Leda
It's about Time
Around Here
The Lost Notebook of Zhao Li
Coming To
Life-Size
The Five Notebooks of Zhao Li
Selected Poems 2002-2021
Years Later
The Dust
A Guide of the Perplexed
For All I Know
The Moon Is the Capital of the World
Piano Music
Enjoy Yourself

The Time of Your Life
The Porch Poems
To Say the Least
A Public Place
True Enough
If You Should See Me Walking on the Road
I, Emily Dickinson and Other Found Poems
Tomorrow, Today and Yesterday
In Short Order
Invisible
Heart's Content
Won't Be Long
Beautiful Day
Peach Girl: Poems for a Chinese Daughter (with Joan
I. Siegel)

ABOUT THE AUTHOR

Nominated for the National Book Award, the Eric Hoffer Book Award, and nominated three times for the Pulitzer Prize, J.R. Solonche is the author of more than forty books of poetry and coauthor of another. He lives in the Hudson Valley.